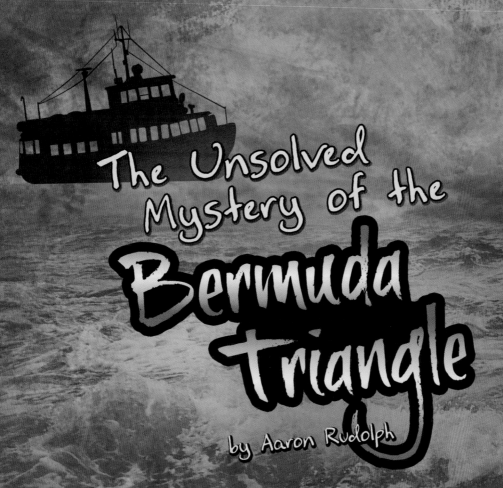

First
Facts®

UNEXPLAINED MYSTERIES

The Unsolved
Mystery of the
Bermuda
Triangle

by Aaron Rudolph

CAPSTONE PRESS
a capstone imprint

First Facts are published by Capstone Press,
1710 Roe Crest Drive, North Mankato, Minnesota 56003
www.capstonepub.com

Library of Congress Cataloging-in-Publication Data
Cataloging-in-publication information is on file with the Library of Congress.
ISBN 978-1-4765-3098-7 (library binding)
ISBN 978-1-4765-3429-9 (eBook PDF)
ISBN 978-1-4765-3443-5 (paperback)

Editorial Credits
Anna Butzer, editor; Juliette Peters, designer; Wanda Winch, media researcher;
Kathy McColley, production specialist

Photo Credits
Capstone: Danielle Ceminsky, 7; Getty Images Inc.: Visuals Unlimited, Inc./Victor Habbick,
4, 18-19, 21; National Archives and Records Administration, 11; Shutterstock: Bojanovic,
boat illustration, maga, cover (lightning), Michael Rosskothen, 17, Nejron Photo, cover, 1,
14, 18 (ocean storm), 8, sgrigor, design element, Vibe Images, cover (boat), zeber, design
element; U.S. Coast Guard (USCG) Historian's Office, 12-13

Printed in the United States of America in North Mankato, Minnesota.
032013   007223CGF13

Table of Contents

Chapter 1

A Strange Disappearance

A big ship sails smoothly toward the Bermuda Triangle. Then the water starts moving faster. Large waves crash against the ship. Suddenly the ship disappears! What happened to it? The Bermuda Triangle is one of the most **mysterious** places in the world.

mysterious—hard to explain or understand

The Bermuda Triangle is in the Atlantic Ocean. The points that make the triangle are Florida, Puerto Rico, and Bermuda. The Bermuda Triangle lies inside these points. Hundreds of boats and planes have **vanished** in this area. Many other ship and plane crews have noticed strange events in the Bermuda Triangle.

Usually no bodies or wreckage from lost ships or planes are found when searching in the Bermuda Triangle.

vanish—to disappear suddenly

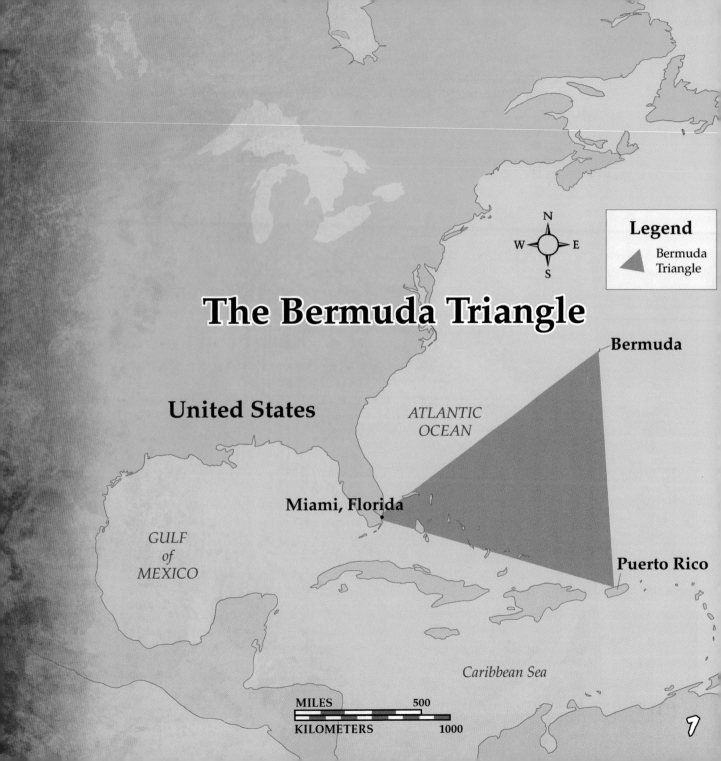

The Bermuda Triangle

Legend

Bermuda Triangle

United States

Bermuda

ATLANTIC OCEAN

GULF of MEXICO

Miami, Florida

Puerto Rico

Caribbean Sea

MILES   500
KILOMETERS   1000

7

Chapter 2

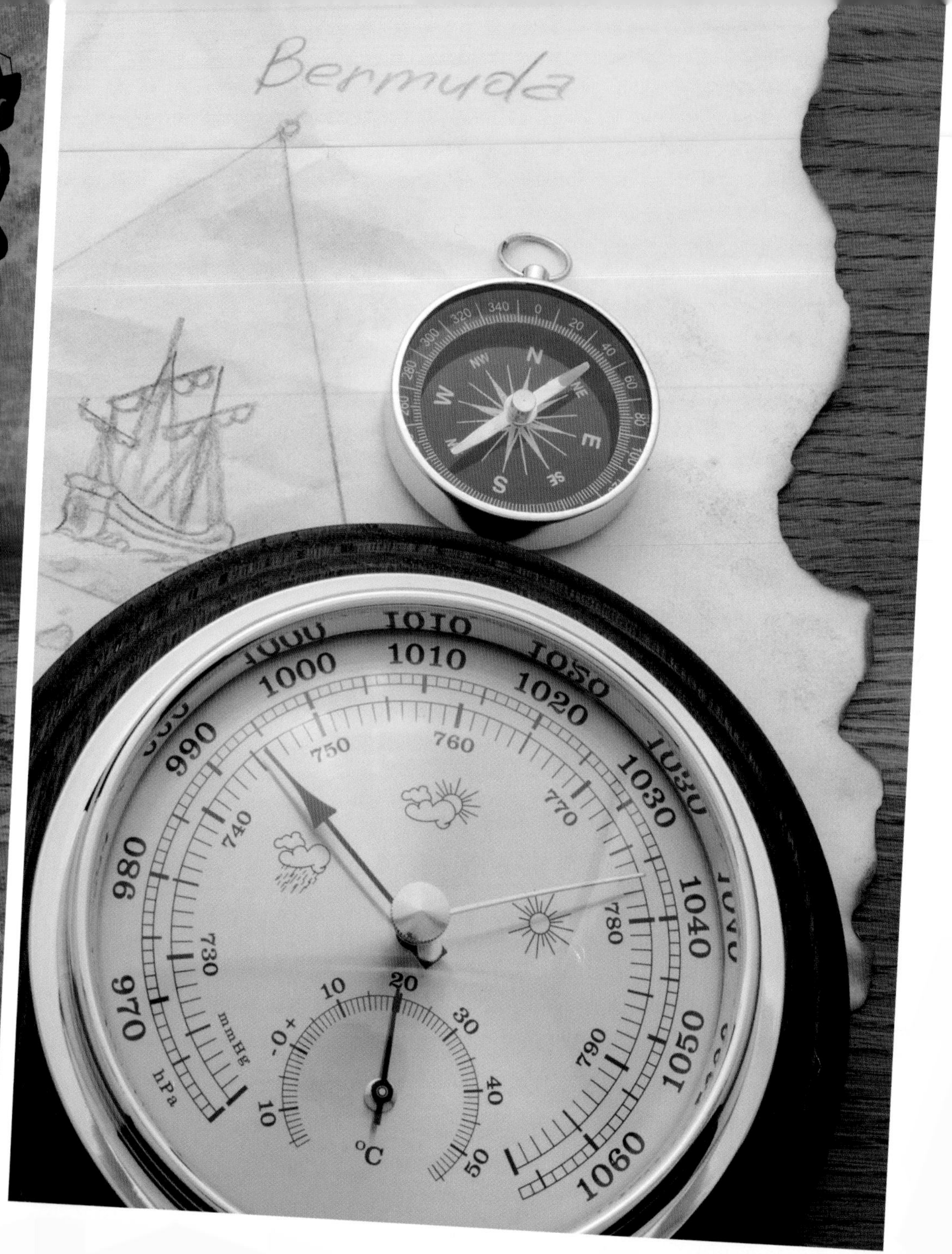

History and Legend

One of the first strange stories about the Bermuda Triangle was told in 1492. Christopher Columbus sailed his ship through the Bermuda Triangle. The crew on Columbus' ship saw a strange light in the sky. Columbus also noticed that his **compass** would not work in this part of the ocean.

compass—an instrument people use to find the direction in which they are traveling; a compass has a needle that points north

There are many stories of planes disappearing in the Bermuda Triangle. One famous story is about five U.S. Navy planes. In 1945 the pilots of the planes became lost and called for help. No one knows what happened to the planes after that. People still want to solve this mystery. They use special cameras to search for them underwater.

The five U.S. Navy planes that disappeared in 1945 are known as Flight 19.

MARINE SULPHUR QUEEN

12

In 1963 the **cargo** ship *Marine Sulphur Queen* was traveling through the Bermuda Triangle. The ship was sailing to Maryland with 39 people on board. Then it vanished. Rescue teams searched for the crew. The crew and the ship are still missing.

About 20 boats disappear in the Bermuda Triangle every year.

cargo—objects carried by a ship, aircraft, or other vehicle

Chapter 3

Studying Clues

Researchers try to explain the events in the Bermuda Triangle. Many people use science to explain the events. Weather in the Bermuda Triangle can change quickly. Clouds and rain can cause crashes by making it hard for people to see. Strong winds can blow small planes off course and make them crash.

researcher—someone who studies a subject to discover new information

True or False?

Do methane gas bubbles cause many of the ship and plane disappearances in the Bermuda Triangle?

True:

Methane gas pockets lie on the ocean floor. When the gas is released, it bubbles to the surface. People believe if a ship gets caught in a gas pocket, it will sink. If the gas reaches high into the air, it could stop a plane engine.

False:

The Bermuda Triangle does not have more methane gas pockets than anywhere else in the ocean.

True:

Researchers have discovered that sometimes one big bubble is created. Other times a bunch of little bubbles are created. There have been tests to see if the bubbles really could sink a ship. The tests lead scientists to believe the bubbles can cause ships to sink.

False:

Some people do not believe that a bubble could cause a large ship to sink.

Some people think there is a **supernatural** reason for events in the Bermuda Triangle. Some people think the area could be a **time warp**. Others believe alien spaceships capture planes and ships in the Bermuda Triangle.

supernatural—something that cannot be given an ordinary explanation

time warp—a place where something from one time is moved to another time in the past or future; time warps have not been proven to exist

Chapter 4

Searching for Answers

Some experts believe the Bermuda Triangle has a strong **magnetic field**. The field can make equipment stop working. Pilots and sailors can become lost if their equipment stops working.

magnetic field—an area of moving electrical currents that affects other objects

Do aliens cause ship and plane
disappearances in the Bermuda Triangle?

True:
  Many ship and
plane crews have
seen strange lights
in the sky above the
Bermuda Triangle.

False:
  Some people believe there are scientific
reasons for these sightings. Falling meteors
can cause bright lights in the sky. Balls of
lightning may appear to follow moving
objects. Sunlight can also reflect off objects
such as weather balloons.

True:
  People have reported
unidentified flying objects
(UFOs) in the Bermuda
Triangle. Some people
believe these UFOs are
alien spaceships.

False:
  Researchers believe
planes, weather balloons,
and birds can be mistaken
for UFOs.

The Bermuda Triangle has interested people for hundreds of years. More than 75 planes and 1,000 boats have disappeared there since the late 1970s. But many other planes and boats have traveled through the area unharmed. Maybe someday we will know what causes the strange events that happen there.

Strong storms can develop quickly in the Bermuda Triangle. Scientists think storms may have sunk many ships in this area.

Glossary

cargo (KAHR-goh)—objects carried by a ship, aircraft, or other vehicle

compass (KUHM-puhss)—an instrument people use to find the direction in which they are traveling; a compass has a needle that points north

magnetic field (mag-NE-tik FEELD)—an area of moving electrical currents that affects other objects

mysterious (miss-TIHR-ee-uhss)—hard to explain or understand

researcher (REE-surch-ur)—someone who studies a subject to discover new information

supernatural (soo-pur-NACH-ur-uhl)—something that cannot be given an ordinary explanation

time warp (TIME WORP)—a place where something from one time is moved to another time in the past or future; time warps have not been proven to exist

vanish (VAN-ish)—to disappear suddenly

Read More

Miller, Connie Colwell. *The Bermuda Triangle: The Unsolved Mystery.* Mysteries of Science. Mankato, Minn.: Capstone Press, 2009.

Stone, Adam. *The Bermuda Triangle.* The Unexplained. Minneapolis: Bellwether Media, 2011.

Troupe, Thomas Kingsley. *The Legend of the Bermuda Triangle.* Legend Has It. Mankato, Minn.: Picture Window Books, 2011.

Internet Sites

FactHound offers a safe, fun way to find Internet sites related to this book. All of the sites on FactHound have been researched by our staff.

Here's all you do:

Visit *www.facthound.com*

Type in this code: 9781476530987

Super-cool stuff!

Check out projects, games and lots more at
www.capstonekids.com

Index